MICHAEL THE ANGEL

By Laura Fischetto / Illustrated by Letizia Galli

A Doubleday Book for Young Readers

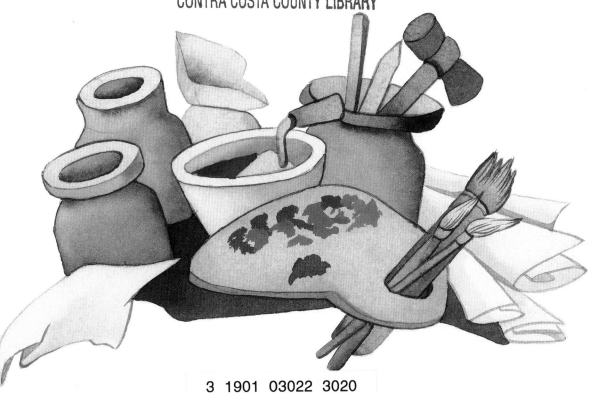

To Chiara and Giulia
—L.F.

To Florence, to Grandpa and Memé
—L.G.

A Doubleday Book for Young Readers
Published by Delacorte Press
Bantam Doubleday Dell Publishing Group, Inc.
1540 Broadway
New York, New York 10036
Doubleday and the portrayal of an anchor with a dolphin are trademarks of
Bantam Doubleday Dell Publishing Group, Inc.
Text copyright © 1993 by Laura Fischetto
Illustrations copyright © 1993 by Letizia Galli

Library of Congress Cataloging in Publication Data
Fischetto, Laura.
Michael the Angel / by Laura Fischetto ; illustrated by Letizia Galli.
p.   cm.
Summary: Examines the life of the noted Renaissance artist and describes how he came to
create some of his greatest works.
ISBN 0-385-30844-2
[1. Michelangelo Buonarroti, 1475-1564. 2. Painters. 3. Painting, Italian.
4. Painting, Renaissance—Italy. 5. Art appreciation.] I. Galli, Letizia, ill. II. Title.
ND623.B9F57   1993   709'.2—dc20
[B]   92-21597   CIP   AC

This book is set in 19-point Weiss
Typography by Lynn Braswell
Manufactured in the United States of America
June 1993
10   9   8   7   6   5   4   3   2   1
BVG

If an angel came down to earth, where would he live? He would probably choose someplace beautiful, someplace famous for its mountains, hills, plains, seas, and cities—someplace like Italy.

Many, many years ago a child was born near Florence,
one of the loveliest Italian cities. His father, Lodovico
Buonarroti, decided to call him Michael the Angel,
which in Italian is Michelangelo.

But what kind of an angel has no wings?

Soon after Michelangelo's birth the Buonarroti
family—father, mother, and their five sons—went to live
in Florence. There Michelangelo's mother died when he
was six. His father tried to be very strict with all the

children but could not make Michelangelo obey. Once
the boy began school he was often in trouble. No matter
how often his teachers scolded him, he would not study.

Florence is a strange and wonderful place—cheerful, but a little rough. Even on sunny days some streets are dark. At times you may feel that someone is spying on you from the little windows of the big houses.

Michelangelo never tired of walking through the city. He looked at the buildings and the tall, narrow towers. He was fascinated by the people too. Sometimes when he stopped to watch them joke and quarrel, he forgot to go on to school. His father had to scold him often.

But what kind of an angel disobeys his father?

Since Michelangelo would not study and would only draw, Lodovico Buonarroti took him to the studio of Domenico Ghirlandaio, where the boy could work as an apprentice and learn everything a painter needs to know. Ghirlandaio was a famous painter, but his studio was very disorderly. Michelangelo's father feared that his son would not learn anything in the midst of such confusion. He thought that being a painter was an odd profession.

Before they could become painters, apprentices had to learn how to make the paints. To produce a certain color, they measured out the right amounts of powder and linseed oil and then mixed them until the shade was just right. Michelangelo learned more each day.

But what kind of an angel was this splattered, multicolored Michelangelo?

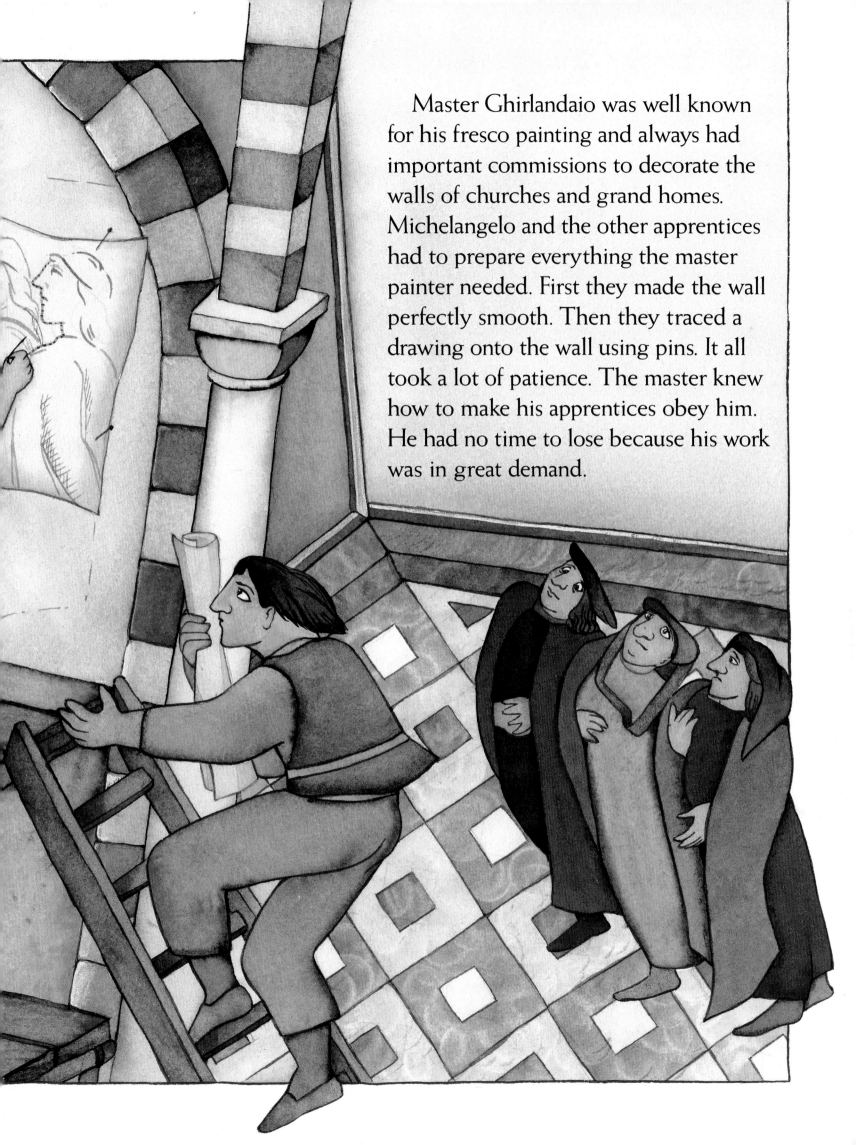

Master Ghirlandaio was well known for his fresco painting and always had important commissions to decorate the walls of churches and grand homes. Michelangelo and the other apprentices had to prepare everything the master painter needed. First they made the wall perfectly smooth. Then they traced a drawing onto the wall using pins. It all took a lot of patience. The master knew how to make his apprentices obey him. He had no time to lose because his work was in great demand.

Michelangelo knew that to become a truly fine artist he would have to learn from the great painters. When he wasn't working, he studied the works of the masters. All the art that made Florence so beautiful was awaiting Michelangelo, and each work had a secret to reveal. Even with so much to study, Michelangelo found the time to quarrel. His friends had to admit that he did not have a good disposition.

Now what kind of an angel
gets his nose broken in a fight?

In Florence there was plenty of work for good painters. All the important people wanted to have portraits of themselves that made them more elegant or taller or thinner or fatter. They would hang them in prominent places in the city. Michelangelo excelled at drawing but had no interest in becoming a great portrait painter. Instead, he decided to leave Ghirlandaio's studio to learn how to sculpt. His father was not pleased.

Lorenzo de' Medici, a merchant prince, was the ruler of Florence at that time. He was also a great supporter of the arts. After seeing Michelangelo's wonderful drawings, he took him to live in his enormous house.

The most famous people of the day, from poets to scientists, were invited to dine at Lorenzo de' Medici's house. Michelangelo listened so carefully to the fascinating guests, he sometimes forgot to eat the fine food.

But what kind of an angel forgets to eat at the table of a prince?

Lorenzo de' Medici wanted to make Florence the most beautiful city on earth. He invited famous master sculptors to teach the young artists of the city. Michelangelo could hardly wait to begin his lessons in sculpting.

In those years Florence was filled with the noise of people quarreling. Michelangelo tried to ignore the noise of the city and worked at his sculpting with great fury. But all the while he dreamed of leaving. He even knew where he wished to go.

Now what kind of an angel was this Michelangelo who was never happy where he was, and always wanted to move on?

Michelangelo went to search for the most beautiful marble in the world for his sculptures. He found it in Carrara, not far from Florence. There, buried in the high mountains, covered with grass and flowers, was beautiful white marble crisscrossed with blue streaks. Men uncovered the stone and cut it into heavy blocks, which were then moved to Florence on wagons or boats. Michelangelo knew he would uncover beautiful sculptures hidden inside those enormous blocks.

Soon everyone saw that Michelangelo was a great artist. He went as far as Rome, where he sculpted the *Pietà*, a huge statue that the whole world admires today. Then he returned to Florence, where he sculpted the gigantic *David* from a single block of marble. As soon as he was finished people began to complain that David's nose was too long. In response, Michelangelo climbed up to the nose, made some noise with his scalpel, and threw powder down on his critics. In truth, the nose remained the same, but everyone thought it had changed. They thanked Michelangelo for having shortened it. The mischievous child had become a mis-chievous man, and he stayed that way all his life.

He was not an angel,
this Michelangelo.
He was just a man.

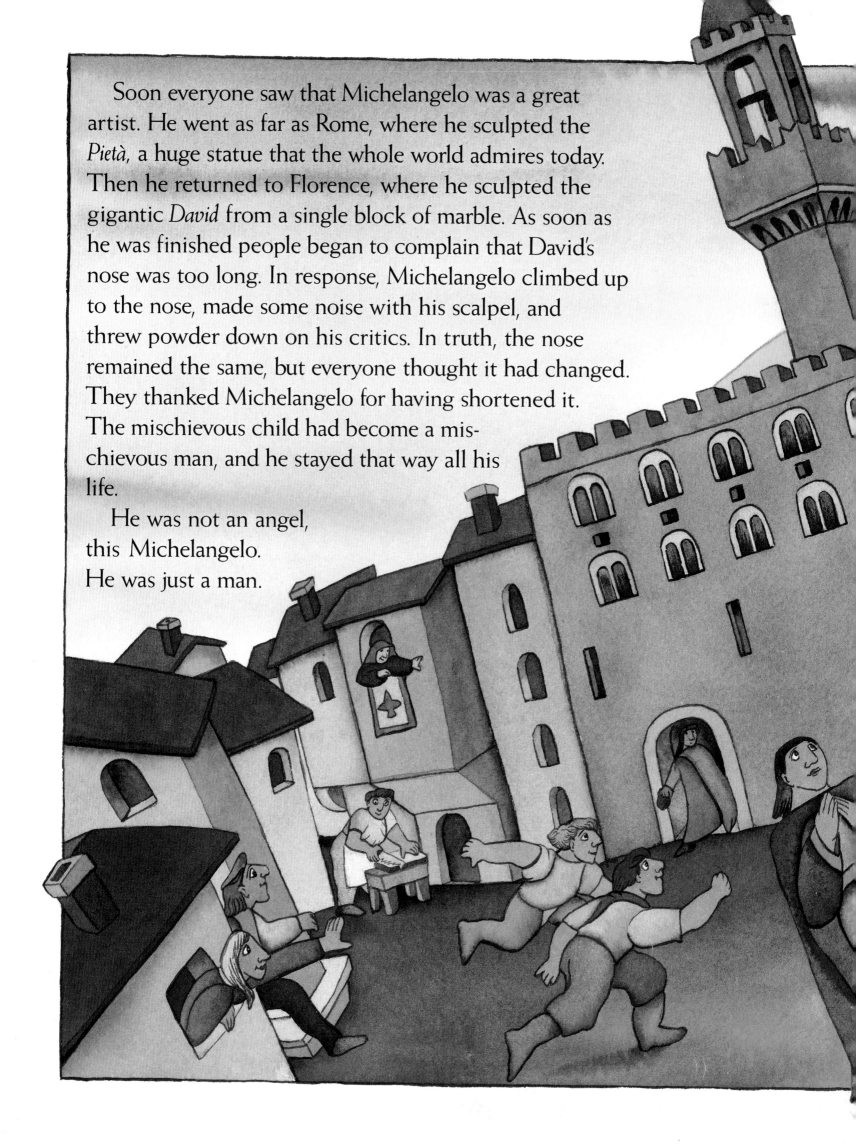

And the angels? We still don't know where they live. But if you take a trip to Italy and look at the marvelous works of Michelangelo, it will probably be as close as you can come on earth to meeting a real angel.

WEST EUROPE

CARRARA

FLORENCE

I T

ROME

GLOSSARY

apprentice—A person who learns an art or skill by working with an expert, such as a *master painter.*

chisel—A metal tool with a sharp edge that is used for shaping a hard surface.

fresco—A picture painted on freshly spread plaster while the plaster is still wet. Frescoes usually decorate walls and ceilings in churches and elaborate houses.

linseed oil—An oil from flaxseed that is used in paint, varnish, ink, and linoleum.

marble—A hard limestone that can be cut, shaped, and polished to make statues, floors, walls, tables, and more.

master painter—A highly skilled artist qualified to teach painting to *apprentices.*

painting—A picture made with paint, such as oil paint, watercolor, or tempera. Paintings are often done on a piece of canvas or on a wall. A person who makes paintings is called a **painter.**

portrait—A painting or drawing or photograph that shows how a person looks.

scalpel—A small, straight, thin-bladed knife sometimes used by *sculptors.*

sculpture—Three-dimensional art that is sometimes carved from stone, welded from metal, or modeled out of clay. A person who makes sculptures is called a **sculptor.**

studio—The working place of a *painter, sculptor,* photographer, or other artist.

Michelangelo was one of the greatest artists the world has ever known. He was born on March 6, 1475, in the small town of Caprese, not far from Florence, Italy, where his family soon moved. The period of history during which Michelangelo lived is known as the Renaissance. Lasting from about 1300 to 1650, it was a time of rediscovery of ancient Roman and Greek art, writing, and thought, which provided tremendous inspiration for artists and thinkers. During Michelangelo's lifetime, Florence was a splendid place to live because it was the artistic capital of Europe.

Although originally trained as a painter in the workshop of Domenico Ghirlandaio, Michelangelo considered himself a sculptor first. His *Pietà* of 1499 in Saint Peter's Church in Rome and his *David* in the city art gallery of Florence are two of his most admired pieces. However, he may be best remembered for the frescoes Pope Julius II persuaded him to paint on the ceiling of the Sistine Chapel in the Vatican, an immense project that took him more than four years to complete. Later in life Michelangelo also became an architect and designed the dome of Saint Peter's Church. He lived and continued to work until February 18, 1564, when he was 88 years old, an unusually ripe old age for a man of the Renaissance.